HAUNTED HISTORY

Waushara Historical Museum

& Old Jail

© 2024 by Scott Bowser

All rights reserved. No part of this book may be reproduced, stored in a retrieval system or transmitted in any form or by any form or by any means without prior written permission by the author.

TABLE OF CONTENTS

Forward..4

Chapter 1

   A Brief History of Wautoma, Wisconsin.......6

Chapter 2

   Welcome to the Waushara Historical Society & Museum..9

Chapter 3

   The History of the Old Jail & Building..........11

Chapter 4

   Stories from Paranormal Investigators.......21

Chapter 5

   Photo Gallery..61

Final Thoughts..81

FORWARD

The Waushara Historical Museum stands as a bastion of history, preserving the rich tapestry of the region's past. Yet, beneath its veneer of antiquity lies a realm of spectral intrigue, where whispers of the past echo through the corridors and shadows dance in the flickering lamplight. Tales of ghostly apparitions and unexplained phenomena have woven themselves into the fabric of the museum's lore, captivating visitors and staff alike.

Some recount encounters with spectral figures wandering the halls, their ethereal forms fading into the darkness as quickly as they appear. Others speak of inexplicable cold spots and eerie sensations that permeate certain rooms, leaving an unsettling chill in their wake. The museum's artifacts, each with their own story to tell, seem to harbor a residual energy that resonates with the spirits of bygone eras.

Among the most infamous tales is that of a phantom lady, said to wander the museum's Victorian parlor, her mournful cries echoing through the night. Legend has it that she is the ghost of a young woman tragically lost to a forbidden love affair, forever trapped in a liminal state between worlds.

Despite the skepticism of some, the real spirits of the Waushara Historical Museum continue to intrigue and mystify those who dare to delve into its haunted history. Whether manifestations of lingering memories or echoes of unfinished business, these spectral presences serve as a reminder that the past is never truly laid to rest.

Chapter One

A Brief History of Wautoma, Wisconsin

Wautoma, Wisconsin, has a nice history dating back to the mid-19th century. Originally inhabited by various Native American Tribes, the area was later settled by European immigrants, predominantly of German and Polish Decent. Wautoma was officially established in 1852 and quickly grew as a logging and farming community due to its fertile soil and abundant timber resources.

The town's economy diversified over time, with the arrival of industries such as dairy farming, cheese production, and tourism, attracted by the area's natural beauty and recreational opportunities.

Today, Wautoma maintains its small-town charm while embracing modern developments and continuing to celebrate its colonial heritage.

In the late 1800's Wautoma experienced significant growth with the construction of railroads, which facilitated transportation of goods and people. The town became a hub for agriculture, particularly dairy farming, and the dairy industry remains a prominent part of the local economy to this day.

During the 20th century, Wautoma continued to evolve, adapting to changes in agriculture and industry. The town also became a popular destination for outdoor enthusiasts, drawn to its numerous lakes, forests, and recreational opportunities such as fishing, hunting, and camping.

In terms of culture and community, Wautoma has preserved its heritage through events like Waushara

County Fair and various festivals celebrating its agricultural roots. The town's historic downtown area still boasts its charming buildings and shops, reflecting its past while also embracing modern amenities.

Back in the early 1900s, Wautoma and Waushara County were kind of like the Wild West, bank robberies, jail breaks, and vigilante justice were very common. In fact, one newspaper referred to the swampy area just north of Wautoma in 1928 as the "Bad Lands" because that is where most of the criminals would hide out. Also, many bank robbers would use the railroad just north of town to escape.

Wautoma has a bit of a dark history. There has been a lot of bloodshed on this ground. Just between the lakes to the east of town, in 1683, there was a battle between 400 Fox (Outagamie) Indians and 1000 Iroquois Indians, there were at least 200 casualties. Around the 1850's, it was no longer only the Indians causing bloodshed between each other. "White Men" came to take their land, and once the Indians were too few to be a threat they fought other white settlers in land feuds.

Overall, Wautoma's history is one of resilience, adaptation, and community spirit, making it unique and a cherished part of Wisconsin heritage.

Chapter Two

Welcome to the Waushara Historical Society & Museum

The Waushara Historical Society & Museum, located at 221 S. Saint Marie St. In Wautoma, Wisconsin, is dedicated to preserving, and sharing the history of Waushara County. Founded in 1962, the Society operates several historic sites and museums, including the Waushara Historical Museum housed in the former county jail, which dates to 1859. The museum featuring exhibits on various aspects of local history, including early settlers, Native American Heritage, agriculture, industry and more.

The society also maintains the Pleasant Lake Schoolhouse Museum, a restored one-room schoolhouse built in 1873, which provides visitors with a glimpse into rural education in the late 19th and early 20th century.

Additionally, the society hosts events, educational programs, and community outreach activities to engage residents and visitors in learning about Waushara County's past.

Through its efforts. The Waushara Historical Society plays a vital role in providing the heritage of the region and fostering appreciation for its cultural and historical significance.

Overall, the Waushara Historical Society serves as a valuable resource for preserving and sharing the stories of the people, places, and events that have shaped the county's history over the years.

Chapter Three

The History of the Old Jail and Building

The Waushara Historical Museum, which was built in 1908 in Gregorian Rival style architecture. It was originally the Waushara County Jail and home to the sheriff. As of today, is the only building in the city of Wautoma on the Historical Register.

Photo Curtesy of Ann Wilkie

The Waushara County Historical Society building stands as a testament to the rich heritage of its community, its walls steeped in the stories of generations past. Originally constructed in the late 19th century, the building served as a hub of activity for the burgeoning town, hosting social gatherings, civic meetings, and cultural events.

Photo Curtesy of Ann Wilkie

Over the years, the building witnessed the ebb and flow of history, weathering the storms of change while remaining a steadfast symbol of community pride. In the early 20th century, it was repurposed as the headquarters of the Waushara County Historical Society, tasked with preserving and celebrating the region's storied past.

Since then, the building has become a beloved fixture of the community, welcoming visitors from near and far to explore its treasures and delve into the annals of Waushara County's history. Its halls are lined with artifacts, photographs, and documents that tell the story of the area's pioneers, settlers, and trailblazers, offering a glimpse into the lives and legacies of those who came before.

Today, the Waushara County Historical Society building stands as more than just a museum; it is a living testament to the resilience and spirit of its community, a place where the past is honored, preserved, and celebrated for generations to come.

As the years passed, the Waushara County Historical Society building underwent renovations and expansions, evolving to meet the changing needs of its community. Its architecture reflects the various eras it has witnessed, from its Victorian roots to its modern-day facade, each layer adding to its character and charm.

Photo Curtesy of Ann Wilkie

Throughout its history, the building has also played a role in local folklore, with tales of ghostly apparitions and unexplained phenomena adding to its mystique. Visitors have reported eerie experiences, from unexplained footsteps echoing in empty corridors to shadowy figures glimpsed out of the corner of the eye.

Photo Curtesy of Ann Wilkie

Despite these spectral whispers, the Waushara County Historical Society building remains a beacon of historical preservation and community pride. Its archives are a treasure trove of knowledge, offering researchers and history enthusiasts alike a wealth of resources to explore.

Today, the building continues to serve as a vital center for community engagement, hosting events, exhibits, and educational programs that celebrate the rich tapestry of Waushara County's past. As it enters its next chapter, the Waushara County Historical Society building stands as a living testament to the enduring legacy of its community and the power of history to inspire and unite us all.

Photo Curtesy of Ann Wilkie

Ed Gein, the infamous serial killer and grave robber, was briefly housed at the Waushara County Jail in Wautoma, Wisconsin, following his arrest in 1957. Gein's crimes, which included the murder of two women and the desecration of numerous graves, shocked the nation and garnered widespread media attention.

After his arrest by authorities from neighboring counties, including the Waushara County Sheriff's Office, Ed Gein was taken into custody and held at the Waushara County Jail while awaiting trial. During his time at the jail, Gein became the subject of intense public fascination, with curious onlookers and journalists flocking to Wautoma to catch a glimpse of the notorious killer.

However, Gein's stay at the Waushara County Jail was relatively brief. In November 1957, he was transferred to the Central State Hospital for the Criminally Insane in Waupun, Wisconsin, where he underwent psychiatric evaluation and treatment. He was later found guilty but criminally insane for the murder of Bernice Worden and spent the remainder of his life confined to mental institutions.

While Ed Gein's time at the Waushara County Jail was short-lived, his case remains one of the most infamous in American criminal history, leaving an indelible mark on the small town of Wautoma and the surrounding community.

Ed Gein outside the Waushara County Jail

During World War II, several German soldiers who were captured by Allied forces were held as prisoners of war (POWs) in various locations across the United

States, including the Waushara County Jail in Wautoma, Wisconsin. The Waushara County Jail was among many facilities across the country that were utilized to detain POWs during the war.

The presence of German POWs in Wautoma and other parts of the United States was part of the broader effort to house and manage prisoners of war following their capture on the battlefield. These POWs were typically held in accordance with the rules and regulations outlined by the Geneva Conventions, which established guidelines for the treatment of prisoners of war.

While held in captivity, German POWs were generally treated humanely and provided with necessities such as food, shelter, and medical care. Many of them were assigned to perform various tasks, such as agricultural work or other labor deemed necessary for the war effort, under the supervision of American authorities.

The presence of German POWs in communities like Wautoma had a significant impact on residents, as it brought a reminder of the global conflict to their doorstep. However, interactions between residents and the POWs varied, with some forming friendships and developing a mutual respect, while others maintained a sense of wariness or suspicion.

After the end of World War II, most German POWs were repatriated to their home country, though some chose to remain in the United States or immigrate to other countries. The period during which German POWs were held in facilities like the Waushara County Jail in

Wautoma remains a fascinating chapter in the history of both the local community and the broader context of World War II.

Chapter 4

Stories from Paranormal Investigators

Thank you all!

I want to extend my deepest gratitude to everyone who generously shared their personal stories and experiences for my book on the Waushara Historical Museum and Old Jail. Your memories and encounters have truly brought the spirit of this historic place to life. This project would not have been possible without your contributions, and I am deeply thankful for your willingness to share your insights and paranormal experiences. Each story adds a unique layer to the rich history of this location, and I am honored to have been able to include them. Thank you all for making this book something special!

Lori McCloud

Curator for the Waushara County Historical Society & Museum

I am the curator of the Waushara County Historical Society & Museum where I have been a volunteer for 24 years. I have experienced a lot of unexplained/paranormal things throughout the years in the former jail & sheriff's living quarters. Here are some of them.

The little girl upstairs, who I call Stella, came when her father was an inmate in jail here. She decided she liked the place and would stay with us.

The little boy, who I call Robert, was a foster child with the family that used to live here. He was given back to his family and died shortly after. He was happy here and stays.

Lila Patterson was a Waushara County dispatcher here for several years. She is my protector and watches over the place.

There is the German kitchen cook who will cook for you (but don't ask for sauerkraut) the phantom smell in the building is too much. Chicken soup or brownies would work.

The deputy in the attic is mean to the spirit children residing there. He visits the furnace room in the basement, too. He also swears at you and tells you to get out.

The upstairs bedroom has either a lady getting ready for a wedding or a man in black I call the doctor. He has been known to shadow crawl on the floor and wall.

The piano teacher that is there does not like you to mess with her piano. If you do not take care, she may pinch or hit you.

There is a doctor that hides in the corner of the doctor's room. He either talks to you or just watches you.

The upstairs jail has Lila or the cook who looks through the food window into the textile room. That is also the rubber room, and she is watching to make sure you are safe.

The upper jail has a German pow soldier that does not like girls in the upstairs jail area. He has been known to push girls out.

Jeb is the one that peeks out of his cell to see what you are doing.

Walter is very friendly to the girls that sit upstairs.

There are many spirits on the outside of the cells. I have had many helpers that have had experiences in the building. There is always something to share.

Lori McCloud

Windigo Paranormal

Founders: Greg & Heather Kelly

My team has visited the Waushara Museum a few times since it's in our home state of WI. An easy hour and half drive from home.

The first time we went there it was blistering hot outside, which in return made the museum even hotter! Ironically just two days later, the museum would have central air installed.

I remember the whole team stepping outside many times during our investigation to get some air because it felt like we were melting! My first investigation there came with much anticipation as I was bringing what I consider one of Wisconsin's national treasures.

I am the owner of one of Ed Geins knives. I had heard the museum had a few of his other artifacts, and my thought process was let's get the gang (Ed's belongings) back together. It's a useful tool for longtime paranormal investigators like me.

Having been a paranormal investigator for 29 years, you pick up a few techniques. I figured this would get the spirits there talking and hopefully one of them being Ed.

Once we put Ed's knife on top of the cupboard his other artifacts are in, we had tons of EMF stuff start going off. What made that interesting was that equipment didn't go off before that the whole time it was placed and running.

I will also note that while holding some of Ed's belongings, one of my investigators got weird. Affected. So much so we asked if he needed to be taken outside to be grounded. He complied and seemed fine the rest of the night.

The second time my team went there was probably my favorite time. Again, I brought Ed's knife with me. While letting those that wanted to hold it and feel its energy, I got one of the clearest class A EVPS ever. It was a man speaking and he said, "my knife severed meat". It was caught in the jail cell that the museum has mocked up to look like the one Ed stayed in.

That night in the jail cell area, we did a second very clear class and evp while we were talking. It was a male and he said, "I'm John". You can imagine my excitement while I was reviewing evidence from that investigation.

Class A evps are those that do not need any electronic device to manifest. I don't claim they are rare, but they kind of are. To receive a class a raw evp so clear, is just all paranormal investigators dream. That and seeing an apparition would be my top two.

I plan to keep investigating the Waushara Museum and bringing Ed's knife back to visit. If it is used in a respectful manner. Being the caretaker of such a thing, it is a responsibility I take very seriously. I

f you ever get the opportunity to investigate the museum, I highly recommend it. After all you will get to me Lori, and she is reason enough to visit there! Lori knows how obsessed with Ed Gein, I am and is always willing to chat away. We bounce theories and facts off one another. It's so fun for me to chat with others who know the gritty details of the infamous Ed Gein.

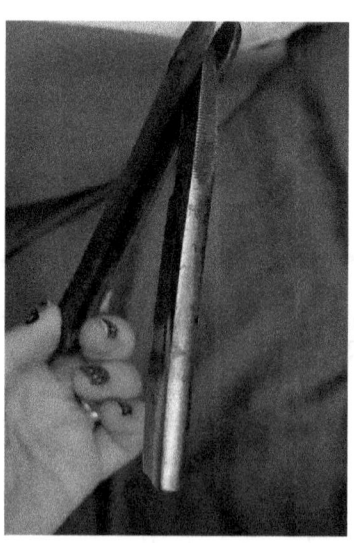 

Ed Gein's Homemade Knife

Greg & Heather Kelly

Greg Kelly

Heather Kelly

We Are Paranormal

Founders: Nathan Hopwood & Mike Minigh

I met Lori, Tom and Dee Dee in 2019. I just went there one day as I heard it was haunted. I did a regular tour and then spoke to Lori about the building. I was there for about two hours chatting about the place and then exchanged information so I could go back to film an investigation there. I was extremely excited to do so. Since then, I have been there many times. I also used to own the Ed Gein knife and skis that are on display there. They are now a part of the museum where they belong. I have so many memories but the things I remember most are the number of times we have gotten Augusta Gein among other spirits to come through. She's not a fan of anyone who wants to communicate with her son. She has gotten to a lot of us and messed us up for a while at times. The energy in that building is always different. I remember on one occasion that we had some amazing evps. One was caught on our camera microphone. when Mike and I were in one of the jail cells. We were setting up and something in a very loud way said get out! Neither Mike nor I reacted to it as we didn't hear it with our own ears. When I went through the footage is when I heard a creepy voice telling us that. That is the same night that Mike got sick and right as he grabbed his stomach someone through the Bugsy Box said, "she's going to make you feel sick." We all heard that in real time. Another team member was in the doorway of the Dr office. She was sitting on the floor, and she moved to the side. As she did that through the bugsy box we heard "Ed No!" To top it off we had a picture of Augusta on the desk of the Dr office. We told her to push her picture down if she didn't like it. Slowly but surely, someone did just that. There was no wind and no breeze going through the office! This place is one of the best haunted locations and like I said I have so many different memories of this place. I look forward to going back very soon!

Nathan Hopwood, Co-Founder We Are Paranormal

Becky Mumm

(Upper Jail)

    I am sending you my experience in the Halloween room. Back in the year of 2017, my friend Julie (Janette) Wagner and I visited the Halloween room around noon on an October day. As we entered the room, the music on the record player/cassette player skipped. And then we heard a loud bang that sounded like a jail cell door slamming shut in the jail area. However, we were the only ones in the museum at the time! There was no one else in the building. We called out for someone to answer us, and no one replied to our call. I do not know if the skipped music and door slamming sound, we heard were a staged effort to scare us, as Bruce Runnels had quite a sense of dry humor. If that is the case, he did a good job at raising the hair on the back of our necks! If our experience wasn't a staged effort, both Julie and I felt an unannounced presence in the museum that October day.

Scott Bowser

A couple years ago while I was researching for my first book Gein, I got to meet Lori at the Waushara Historical Museum & Old Jail.

Lori told me stories about the many spirits that are there. I was intrigued but was skeptical about whether I believed her or not. This was a time in my life I did not believe in spirits.

As time went on, I got invited to my first paranormal investigation at the museum by Sara Evraets and Kalina Marie Schira. The most memorable part of the night was when Kalina was using dousing rods in Ed Gein's cell. We were getting some activity but at the end of the night I still felt skeptical.

I was invited to another Investigation by Nathan Hopwood. Little did I know that this would be the night that made me a believer.

We were in the upper jail and Nate had his bugsy box going and asking questions. Nate introduced us to the spirits. One question that Nate asked the spirits if they could say our names and right after that I heard "Scott, Scott, Scott" and then I heard the name "Nate" come from the bugsy box. Chills went through my body, and it was at that moment I was a full-fledged believer.

Another story and probably my most favorite experience happened when I was an investigator with a paranormal group. There were four of us investigating that night.

In the attic there's the spirits of two children, Sally and Robert, and a spirit we call the deputy.

We had our rim pod out and voice recorders going and cat balls on the floor. Our rim pod kept going off, so we felt the children were having fun and were active.

While sitting in the chair I asked the children if one of them could touch me. Just after I asked that I felt a cold finger touch my hand by my thumb.

This was by far the best night I ever had investigating to this point. I look forward to many more investigations at the museum.

WISP

Rachael Kuklis Zimmerman

All right, so the first thing I got to tell you is I'm not big into like serial killers or Ed Gein, so I didn't really know much about this Museum. After the investigation at the Museum is when things started to happen.

A few days later after work I went to my hair appointment, I was coming home around between 5:30 6:00, somewhere as I was just coming into Princeton my radio started to be all staticky on the station. I was like losing reception for just a Split Second as I looked at the radio station and I glanced up into the rear mirror, I see a man sitting in the backseat of my car.

The man had dark combed hair, it looked slick, his eyes were small and squinty, and his face was long and skinny. It startled me and I remember getting closer to the steering wheel and driving a little bit faster to get home.

When I looked back into the rearview mirror, he was gone. I then thought maybe it was just my imagination. I thought, well maybe the streetlight. It was just a shadow but the more I thought about it at home the details that I could remember were so real.

While I was in the car, I do remember feeling like someone was touching a certain spot by my head. It was like a tingly sensation, and it was only in that one spot.

I didn't tell anyone right away, until things started to affect me more. A few days after that happened, I would have random spots that the energy would be different in my house, knocking on my little doors like little taps.

The taps by my wall were at times where I would hear footsteps coming into her bedroom and I thought it would be the kids coming into our bedroom, but nothing.

That is when I knew I needed Michelle to help me, she is a sensitive like me. That is when I started to see images of things.

I remember writing them all down and then relaying them to Dave and the rest of the team about what was happening. The images that I remember seeing were a vanilla folder like it was an old wrinkly folder against concrete blocks like a wall.

I remember seeing a white door like I needed to go through this white door. Then this male kept showing me what I needed to do. I asked Dave if we could go back to the museum, I needed to put the puzzle pieces together.

We set up a time with Lori and we went down, just a small group of us. I think there were only three of us that went during the week. We set up a few cameras and I do think maybe we have some recordings of this, but I knew this person was from down in the basement by Charlie's room.

I went back to why I think this man or spirit came with me. I want to say it was like where the military room or by the research room.

I remember staring out of the room looking over where they had the computers. There was a red monitor there, it was a monitor with a red light going and I saw something moving over there and blocking the red light and I I knew I felt somebody was there watching us and I almost wonder if it was him.

Anyways we did the investigation again down there trying to find this folder, I knew what I was looking for, I just couldn't find it until I saw the white door. I have never even seen that white door before. I remember asking Lori what's in that room and it was locked, and we went into that room and it's like a room with tons of paper and some really old stuff, I knew I was being drawn to.

There's another room that you got to go into and then there was some shelving with some random stuff. There I saw the brick wall and there's the vanilla envelope. We opened the vanilla envelope. There was a VHS videotape, and I don't still to this day have no idea if this was him.

There was no picture, and nobody had a VHS to watch it. All I do know is that Lori put it on her desk and when I asked her a few days later if she found out anything, she said that the envelope went. To this day I still never found out if it was him. I truly hope whoever the male is that he's at peace and he's able to come and go wherever he is, but I will never know.

Here is a story about the children. Now we know that there were children in the Attic in the investigation, a boy and a girl. I don't exactly know when these little visitors started showing up at my house.

I have two kids, a boy and a girl. One day my 9-year-old daughter told me that she saw a little girl standing in her closet, she described this girl as in a dress or nightgown. She said it looked like pajamas and she couldn't tell if her hair was dark or blonde.

Another time she swore that she thought her brother was going into her room which you know how siblings are, they don't want them in the room. She went in there to go yell at him and it wasn't him and there was nobody in that room. She swore she saw this boy who looks like Gavin running in her room. I didn't go too much into it with her afraid of maybe being scared.

There was another occasion where she had said her clothes would be moving in the closet, her hangers would click against each other. I was just assuming that it could have been the heat vent blowing air.

It wasn't until we went back to the museum with the team with everything that we caught. We did an interview to show them the videos and stuff like that. We went back up into the attic and when I went up in that attic, I knew right away I pictured a yellow truck like a dump truck that lights up and the style right away images in my head. I knew then I was like these children are asking for something and it took me a couple days later I found the doll that was buried in Ava's closet. She had like a laundry basket, it was the last doll in the basket I didn't even know where she got this, it was like a rag doll.

I have no idea, and I had a hunt down this yellow truck in my son's room because I figured if I could give the children spirits these toys maybe they'll stop coming to my kids. A few days later I went back there and asked Lori, "can I please give these toys to the Attic?"

Trust me it took me a lot of guts to go up in the attic by myself in the daytime and just put them down somewhere and so far, so good. I don't think we ever experienced those children again at my home. I just remember asking them not to harm my children and do not scare them, and it's been quiet since.

I still wonder occasionally about the male that was in my vehicle and how is he, where is he now and are the children happy and are they okay.

What I don't like was I did see was a YouTube clip of some sort, but I did not like this male who was doing a ghost hunt there and using a Ouija board. You're just asking for trouble, the spirits, they just need peace not Danger.

Phantasm Paranormal

By Danielle Kossow

What more can I say about the Waushara Museum other than it is such an amazing place! Not only the activity of the amazing spirits that reside there, but the history itself. The moment I walked into those doors I instantly fell in love with it there. There is never a time that my team (Phantasm Paranormal) and I spend the day/night at the museum and never get any bit of activity. We have had so many amazing things happen while there it is hard to only choose one!

One particular favorite part of the museum of mine is the upstairs jail. In particular the very last jail cell on the left side is where I have my most experiences and the one place I seem to always be called to. Here resides a German soldier that is usually known to be mean to individuals who come to visit, especially women. He is known for pushing them down, giving them negative feelings, as well as choking them, often to the point where women feel as if they are being suffocated. Due to this fact there is a rule that no women can be in the upper jail area without any men. However, my experiences that I have up there are far from anything negative. I've never felt anything harmful coming from there. Each and every time I go upstairs to the German Soldiers cell I get a happy and calm feeling more so than a scared or worried feeling. Whenever we set up any equipment up there, no matter what it is, (even though the favorites of his seem to be a simple cat ball or rem pod) it almost always instantly starts going off, especially for me when I'm on the cell with him.

Almost every time I state I am going to leave or go out of the cell the rem pod will instantly go off as if he is trying to say that he does not want me to leave. If I do happen to exit the cell the rem pod will continually go off until I step foot back into the cell and he will back away and stop the rempod. He commonly will also make it go off or on, on my demand, which doesn't normally happen with anyone else. Often times when a teammate and I sit up in the cell on the bed and turn a spirit box up the German soldier often comes through, or we like to think it is him, because we get the same voice every time that has a German accent. There have even been times we hear German words come through. However, in order for this experience to routinely happen there must not be many others up there with me. He tends to only like to communicate with me when it's myself and only a couple of others.
I'm not exactly sure why he tends to like me more than anyone else and why my experiences with him are so much more than most people, especially friendly ones vs. Negative or angry ones. Sometimes I tend to think it is because I am in fact German and Hungarian and know a little bit of German language, which perhaps

makes him feel more at ease or comfortable around me, or maybe it's just my overall demeanor, being calm and quieter. Because of the experiences I've had with him, as well as never getting any harmful feelings towards me, his name to me has now became my "boyfriend" the German soldier by my teammates.

Another amazing experience I have had in the upstairs jail, (the whole upstairs in itself, no particular one area), was when my team and I had all sorts of equipment set up throughout the whole upstairs area and each and every piece of equipment up there went off and continued to go off for a good 30/40 minutes. No one could believe what we were seeing and hearing with our own eyes. Even my 360 puck that is always set up in front of the stairways in the main doorway was going nuts. It was red almost the whole entire time, flashing, and making noise, which means someone was standing practically on top of it the whole time as it is motion activated and will only turn red for a slight second and then have a white light come on wherever the motion occurred.

Overall, there is never a dull moment while visiting the Waushara Museum. It is one of my favorite places to investigate, not only because of the activity that always happens there, but because of the homey feeling I get each and every time I'm there. This is a place I highly suggest you visit if you haven't already been there, it surely will not disappoint.

Danielle Kossow- Team Member of Phantasm Paranormal

Jay DeLap

The first time we ever went to the jail/museum we went with Phantasm Paranormal on their first visit too , it was registered under Ann's name so nobody from the museum knew who the other guests were or where they were from.

We investigated quite a while that night and when Aaron and some of the team went down into the basement conference room to eat, I stepped in to tell them about an experience in the attic.

When on the ledge along the wall I noticed a manilla folder full of photocopied obituaries waiting to be clipped and filed and when I stepped closer, I noticed two of them sitting out away from the folder. I lifted the first one up and the second one was one of my grandmother who had passed like 2 yrs before. So, we knew it wasn't a fresh addition nor did anyone there know I was on the guest list, Lori and Tom had no idea or why those 2 were sitting out either.

Paranormal Party

By JamieLynn Keller

Here is my story of my time last June of 2024 at the Waushara Historical Museum and Old Jail.

This night I was teaming up with Crossingaurd Paranormal and Hannah for our investigation. Tom and Lori were on site to welcome us to the museum as they always do.

We first went into the jail section and set up our equipment. We didn't get much activity at first but when we came back later, we did get some rem pod activity and a few evps, one being male saying "Get Out".

In the school room we set up our equipment and we ended up getting multiple evps of someone saying, "It's you" and "You tell me" And also one saying, "Oh my god yes, it is, it won't work".

Tom did take us over to the old school building a short distance from the museum. There we caught an evp of someone saying the name "Dan". We also had our proximity sensor going off by the door.

We went back to the museum and while we were upstairs Christian and Hannah seen a male shadow figure between the kids' room and music room.

We had an amazing investigation as always at the museum. I enjoy coming here I so much that I have been here many times and will continue to come back.

JamieLynn Keller

WTL

By Lauren Twardzik

On March 16th, 2024, we were invited to investigate the Old Waushara County Jail. We had heard a lot about the jail, and we were excited to see what evidence we would get.

The 3 of us invited my cousin Lily, and her boyfriend. Lily's boyfriend who was a skeptic before the jail had mentioned his doubts about the paranormal. The 3 of us have been investigating for a few years now and we let him, and Lily know that evidence was never guaranteed. The important thing was to keep an open mind.

We arrived at the jail and began our tour. The location is beautiful and historic. We were incredibly impressed with how detailed each room was. As the tour guide took us through the home section of the location, we made our way towards the second floor, into what was known as the "Doll Room". In a single file line, we began exiting the room. As we exited and moved towards the kitchen, the door to the attic (which had been wide open the entire tour) slammed shut right in front of us. As we all stood there in shock, we immediately tried to think of ways to debunk what had just happened. Throughout the night, we tested the door over and over again. Checking for wires, drafts, mechanics, etc. To this day, we are unable to debunk what had happened and, in that moment, my cousin's boyfriend, no longer identified as a skeptic.

Throughout the rest of the night, we had multiple pieces of equipment light up in intelligent ways. Conversations with the soldier in the second-floor cells were active. Physical feelings such as touching, choking sensations, and back pain started to happen to Lily, Tais, and I. Bells were being rung on their own and figures were being captured on the SLS camera, outside the nurse's office door.

Our night at Waushara County Jail was incredible. We all walked away from the location with some sort of paranormal experience. We talk about our time there till this day and can't wait to eventually make a return. We are grateful for Phantasm Paranormal for making the experience so comfortable and fun.

WTL- Tais, Lauren and Wiktoria

Tom Goetz

My name is Tom Goetz, president of the Waushara County Historical Society & Museum. When I first started volunteering at the museum I was told about the spirits that reside in the building. My reaction to that was, "either you help me work or stay out of my way." I have had several things happen while in the building, here are a few of my experiences.

1) While I was with Nate & Abby from the group We Are Paranormal, the 3 of us were upstairs walking in the hallway just coming out of the children's bedroom. On the spirit box was "That was rude"! I replied, "I'm sorry, we forgot to thank them."

2) As I was placing a fan to dry the carpet that we had just cleaned and before I even turned the fan on,
The door to the children's bedroom started to close. Figuring they didn't want the fan there, I moved it to a different areas for them.

3) As I was working up in the attic, I moved the children's toys to the side, out of the way of the ladder. When I returned the next day, they were all moved back to where they originally were!

4) I set up a camera in the attic facing where the kids seem to play hoping to catch some activity. One early morning I was alerted to activity, and I watched as the camera was moved away from the kid's play area and faced a different direction.

Char Stratton

I was cleaning the dining room and saw a black coat going upstairs. I asked Lori who it was, and she told me about the Dr across the street. . .I'm glad I haven't seen more.

Lori also showed me on her phone a little boy up in the attic getting something.

Hannah Fredrick

My first experience was Tom had just finished giving us a tour and we were figuring out where we were going to start investigate for the evening, I was in the booking room when I happened to look down the hall where they have the general store set up when I had seen a woman in a flowy white dress go from the doorway into the now dining room area, and initially I had thought well maybe it was Tom checking things out back there when I happened to turn around to see Tom was outside with everybody else, so I went looking to see if anyone was down there and nobody was there and they didn't make a sound when they walked away either, and a lot of those floors squeak upon walking anywhere.

The second experience I had was on the second floor, and as I was walking up the steps, I had asked Jamie if she could smell Sauerkraut? To which the smell followed us down the hallway, and had gotten more intense as we were huddled at the end of the hallway, to which I had asked again if anybody else could smell Kraut? And Chris could then also smell it, so him and I walked down to the kitchen and the smell dissipated upon walking down the hallway by the kitchen, and then we came back to where we had been standing and there was still the smell of kraut, and as Chris had turned to tell Jamie about and turned to look back at me, he had seen a woman in a dress standing next to me and just as fast as she was their she was gone. The dress I had seen the female spirit wearing earlier is on the second floor which threw me for a loop. I very much look forward to going back and investigating more but so far those are my main two experiences in the museum.

Glenn Balistreire

We were Investigating the holding cell (aka the railroad room) during a Facebook live event when all of a sudden, my name started getting called out through the spirit box. I walked over to the table that the spirit box was sitting on and then the SLS started going crazy with a stick figure trying to climb on my back.

The spirit box started a conversation with me in a very familiar female voice calling me bro. They turned off the Facebook live event because it became very personal as soon as my wife, my daughter, and I figured out who was coming through to me.

It was my adopted sister who had died a few weeks prior. Her death was under investigation. I asked her what happened, and she told us that she did it, and she was sorry. It was about 3 weeks late, and I get phone call from her daughter, and she tells me that the police report came back about what happened to her mom. It stated that my sister committed suicide. I told her that I knew she did it, and she asked how I knew it.

I had her come over and I played the video from that night, and she started to cry, saying that's my mom's voice before we even started asking the questions to verify that it was her.

I am a trigger object for the German solder upstairs in the jail house. Every time I am anywhere in the jail the German soldier is more active than normal. I had my phone going with a German to English translation alongside a spirit box and held a conversation with him for about 15 minutes.

I am also a person that Agusta likes apparently. I can always get her to come through on both the SLS and the spirit box when I am in the holding cell. I have had her yelling at people I was with, but when I started talking to her, she was very pleasant and kind to me. She has even said my name few times, even when I wasn't investigating. I would have my wife or daughter come and find me just to tell me that a German accented ladies is saying my name.

Phantasm Paranormal

By Ann Wilkie

On February of 2024, I was investigating the museum with my teammates of Phantasm Paranormal. Megan and I decided to go into the lower jail by ourselves to see if anyone wanted to communicate. We set up our equipment all the way around the cells and things immediately started going off. "Hi. Thank you for letting us know you are here." I said. Megan asked "who is here with us"? I sat down on the cot as Megan poked her head out of the cell to look around. "I just saw a shadow" she said. "I'm sitting so it's not my shadow!" I told her. She laughed and said it was way up on the wall and sure, now they come out to play since the night is winding down!!

At this time, all the equipment that we had put all the way around the cells was going off like crazy and Megan was watching from the doorway of the cell. "Who is in here? Are you upset that we are in your cell"? I asked. Still, the equipment continues to trigger on both sides of the cell block. Megan grabs a SLS cam and peeks her head out. "Hello? Anyone here want to talk to us?" "We mean no disrespect by sitting in here" I said. "I kind of want to put the dead bell out in the hallway and see what happens" Megan said and grabbed it out of the case. "I'm coming out to place this item in the hallway on the floor.

You can ring it by touching it or just by getting close to it" she says as she rings it to show the spirits. "Augusta? Are you here with us?" The flux turns red so no. "Ed? Are you here?"

At this time, Megan (who is still standing in the doorway of the cell) turns the SLS towards me and says that there is someone sitting next to me on the cot. "Is that you Carl?" Megan asks. "Can you ring that bell in the hall? We think we've seen you a couple times and appreciate you setting off our other devices. We would love it if you could ring the bell for us too." I said.

"We will stay in the cell. We will not chase you; we will not harm you. You are welcome to move around." Megan sits on the cot next to me with the SLS and the figure is still in the cell and a second one appears. "Do you like having women in your cell?" Megan asked. "If one of you is Carl, can you please raise your hand?" "Is whoever being out in the hallway in here with us now?" At this time, we decided to try another device and got out a spirit box. We also brought out a Bible. "Would you like me to read from the Bible to you?" I asked. A flux turned green, and I started reading A Prayer for Justice.

When I was finished, "Amazing" came through the spirit box. The equipment kept going off like a spirit was doing laps around the jail cells. Megan poked her head back out of the cell and looked towards the door going into the building. "I just saw a shadow again! Whoa!" as she came back into the cell. "Encounter" came over the spirit box. "Yes, she encountered you!" I laughed. I was still sitting on the cot and felt electricity like I was being touched. Megan pointed the SLS in my direction. "Yup, someone is next to you and touching you right where you are feeling it!" We kept asking for more information or a name to figure out who we were talking to but with no luck. It started to quiet down. At this time, our investigation time was ending, and it was time to head out. "Goodnight, everyone. Thank you for interacting with our devices and for talking to us. We'll see you next time!" we said as we headed out for the night.

Ann Wilke & Megan Seager

Chapter 5

Photo Gallery

I would like to extend my deepest gratitude to Ann Wilke for her invaluable contribution to this book. Her dedication and skill in capturing the essence of the Waushara Historical Museum & Old Jail through her photography have truly brought the stories within these walls to life. Each photo serves as a powerful visual connection to the past, allowing readers to experience the rich history and lingering spirits that inhabit this historic site.

Ann's keen eye for detail and her ability to convey the unique atmosphere of the Museum and Old Jail have added an irreplaceable dimension to this work. Her photographs not only complement the narrative but also stand as a testament to the enduring significance of these locations. Thank you, Ann, for your passion, your artistry, and for sharing your talents so generously with this project. Your work has made this book a more vivid and engaging journey into the history and hauntings of the Waushara Historical Museum & Old Jail.

Waushara Historical Society

Upper Jail

Upper Jail

Upper Jail

Upper Jail

Upper Jail

Record Room

Up Stairs Kitchen

Up Stairs Kitchen

Sports Room

Sewing Room

Second Floor Master Bedroom

School Room

Railroad Room

Kids Room

General Store

Sewing Room

Attic

Doctors Office

First Floor Jails

Dining Room

Entrance to the Parlor

Parlor

Research Room

Apparition of German Soldier in Upstairs jail.

Photo courtesy of East Oxford Paranormal,

David Bignell

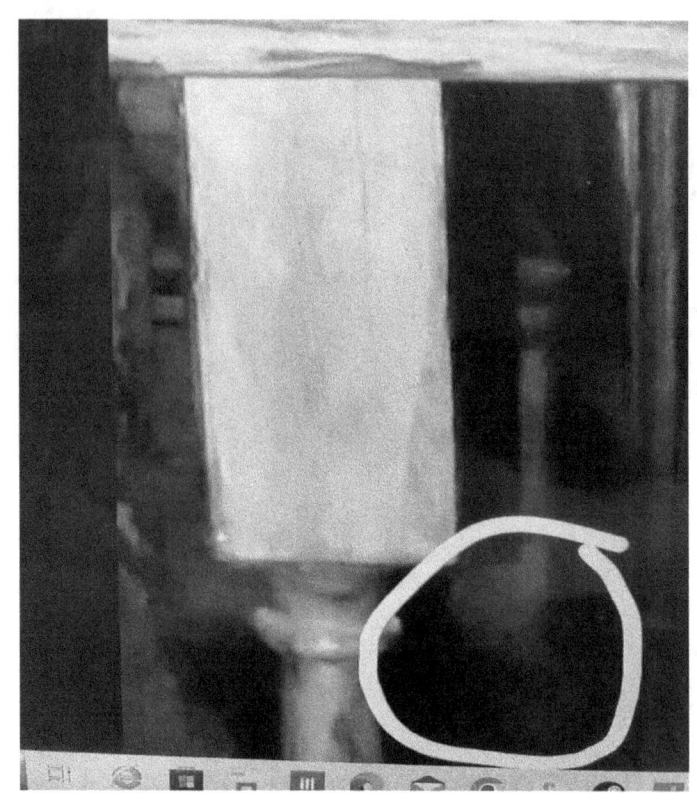

Apparition of "Sally" on the stairs by the Parlor.

Photo courtesy of East Oxford Paranormal,

David Bignell

Final Thoughts

As we reach the conclusion of our journey through the haunted corridors and eerie past of the Waushara Historical Museum & Old Jail, it is impossible not to feel the weight of history and the lingering presence of those who once walked these halls. This book has aimed to delve deep into the layers of history, uncovering the stories of those who lived, worked, and, in some cases, suffered within these walls. The tales of hauntings, ghostly apparitions, and unexplained phenomena are not just remnants of folklore, but they serve as a reminder of the human experiences tied to this place—both the ordinary and the extraordinary.

The Waushara Historical Museum & Old Jail is more than just a building; it is a portal to the past, where the echoes of history refuse to fade away. From the chilling accounts of shadowy figures spotted in the dead of night to the unexplained sounds that have sent shivers down the spines of many visitors, this place stands as a testament to the belief that some things, and some spirits, are simply too strong to be confined to history books.

One of the most fascinating aspects of exploring a location like the Waushara Historical Museum & Old Jail is the intersection of fact and folklore. The history of the jail is well-documented, with records of inmates, jailers, and the various functions it served over the years. Yet, it is the stories that exist in the shadows, passed down through generations, that truly captivate the imagination. The blend of documented history with the mysterious and the supernatural gives this place its unique character—a character that has been preserved through the efforts of the Waushara County Historical Society and the dedicated individuals who continue to keep these stories alive.

Throughout the writing of this book, it became clear that the hauntings of the Waushara Historical Museum & Old Jail are not just about the presence of ghosts or spirits; they are about the lingering energy of the past. Every creak of the floorboards, every cold draft, every inexplicable sound can be traced back to a time when this building was full of life—sometimes vibrant, sometimes tragic. The stories of those who were imprisoned here, whether they were guilty or wrongfully accused, contribute to the heavy atmosphere that many have reported feeling. The jail was a place of confinement, punishment, and, in some cases, despair, and those emotions have seemingly seeped into the very fabric of the building.

But this place is not solely defined by its darker moments. The Waushara Historical Museum & Old Jail also tells the story of a community—its resilience, its growth, and its dedication to preserving its heritage. The transformation of the old jail into a museum is a testament to the value that the people of Waushara County place on their history. It is a space where the past is not forgotten but instead is honored and remembered. The museum now stands as a bridge between the living and the dead, between history and the present, offering a unique opportunity to explore the rich tapestry of life that has unfolded within its walls.

The stories of hauntings are, in many ways, reflections of the people who once inhabited these spaces. Whether it's the spirit of a long-forgotten prisoner, a former jailer who still keeps watch, or an unidentified presence that seems to drift through the halls, these hauntings remind us that history is never truly behind us. It lingers, it influences, and sometimes, it makes itself known in ways that defy explanation.

As you close this book, consider the significance of preserving not just the physical structure of the Waushara Historical Museum & Old Jail, but also the stories that come with it. Every ghost story, every whispered legend adds another layer to the rich history of this place. By sharing these tales, we keep the memory of those who came before us alive, and we acknowledge the profound impact that the past has on the present.

In writing *Haunted History: Waushara Historical Museum & Old Jail in Wautoma, Wisconsin*, I have sought to balance the historical with the supernatural, the documented with the whispered. It is my hope that readers come away with not only a deeper understanding of the history of this unique location but also an appreciation for the mysteries that continue to surround it. The blend of truth and legend, of fact and fear, creates a narrative that is as compelling as it is unsettling. It challenges us to question what we know, what we believe, and what might still be lurking just out of sight.

Ultimately, this book serves as a reminder that history is never static. It is dynamic, ever-changing, and, in some cases, ever-present. The Waushara Historical Museum & Old Jail is a place where the past is palpably alive, where history is not just remembered but experienced. Whether you are a believer in the paranormal or a skeptic, there is no denying the powerful sense of history that pervades this place. And perhaps, after reading this book, you too will feel a deeper connection to the stories, the people, and the spirits of the Waushara Historical Museum & Old Jail.

Thank you for joining me on this journey through the haunted history of Waushara County. As you set this book down, remember that the past is never far behind us, and in places like the Waushara Historical Museum & Old Jail, it might be closer than you think.

About the Author

Scott E. Bowser is the author of six non-fiction books, Gein (2021), The Travelers Guide to Ed Gein (2021) and The Ed Gein Chronicles (2023), Wisconsin Ghostly Legends (2024) & Blood in the Heartland (2024) & Whispers in the Walls (2024). Scott appeared on MGM Plus TV show "Psyco: The Lost Tapes of Ed Gein"

Scott was born in 1964, in Kingsford, Michigan and lived his young years in Neenah, Wisconsin. Scott always had an interest in true crime and the paranormal whether it be reading about it or watching it on tv.

Scott now lives in Wisconsin Rapids. Wisconsin where in his spare time he gives Ed Gein tours in Plainfield, Wisconsin. Scott also in his spare time creates children and adult coloring books which all are also available on Amazon. He is currently writing a screenplay for his first book "Gein".

Other Books by Scott Bowser

Available on Amazon & Barnes and Noble

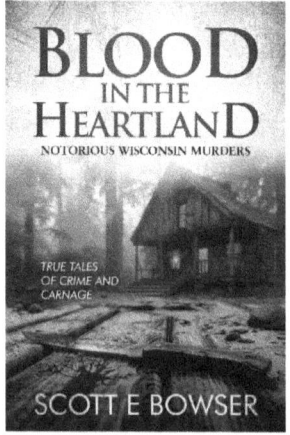

 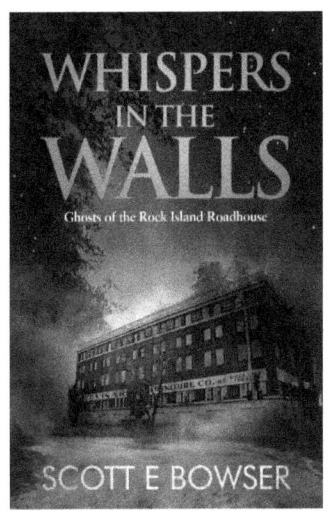

www.ingramcontent.com/pod-product-compliance
Lightning Source LLC
LaVergne TN
LVHW012033060526
838201LV00061B/4581